LET'S CELEBRATE

Harriet Tubman

and Black History Month

by Polly Carter

pictures by Brian Pinkney

Silver Press

Produced by Kirchoff/Wohlberg, Inc.
Text copyright © 1990 Kirchoff/Wohlberg, Inc.
Illustrations copyright © 1990 Brian Pinkney and
Kirchoff/Wohlberg, Inc.

Published by Silver Press, a division of Silver Burdett Press, Inc.
Simon & Schuster, Inc., Prentice Hall Bldg., Englewood Cliffs, NJ 07632

Printed in the United States of America

10   9   8   7   6   5   4   3   2

Library of Congress Cataloging-in-Publication Data
Carter, Polly.
Harriet Tubman and Black History Month / by Polly Carter:
pictures by J. Brian Pinkney.
p. cm.—(Let's celebrate)
Summary: Examines the experiences of the runaway slave who risked
her life to help others through the Underground Railroad.
1. Tubman, Harriet, 1820?-1913—Juvenile literature 2. Slaves—
United States—Biography—Juvenile literature. 3. Afro-Americans—
Biography—Juvenile literature. 4. Afro-Americans—Anniversaries,
etc.—Juvenile literature. 5. Underground railroad—Juvenile
literature. [1. Tubman, Harriet, 1820?-1913. 2. Slaves. 3. Afro-
Americans—Biography. 4. Underground railroad.] I. Pinkney, J.
Brian, ill. II. Title. III. Series.
E444.T82C37 1990   89-49538
305.5′67′092—dc20   CIP
[B]   AC
ISBN 0-671-69115-5   ISBN 0-671-69109-0 (lib. bdg.)

LET'S CELEBRATE

Harriet Tubman

and Black History Month

Life as a Slave

"I'll run away," cried Harriet.

"*Shh!*" whispered another slave. "Miss Susan will hear you. Then she'll whip us both."

"She just did whip me," said Harriet. Hot tears ran down her cheeks. "She whipped me for not dusting her table the right way."

"Don't let Miss Susan see you cry. She'll whip you again," said the other girl. "You're her slave now. She can do anything she wants. She pays your master. So you have to work for her now."

Harriet's master had sent Harriet to work for Miss Susan. Harriet missed her family. She felt sad and lonely.

"Here—you!" Miss Susan said to Harriet. "Put the baby to bed."

One of Harriet's jobs was to rock the baby's cradle all night. If she stopped, the baby would wake and cry. Then Harriet would be whipped.

Harriet rocked the cradle. She closed her eyes. She could almost see her mother and father working in the cornfield at home.

Harriet's eyes flew open. Had she fallen asleep? Almost. Harriet stood up just in time to hand the baby to Miss Susan. It was morning.

Harriet was very hungry. There was a bowl of sugar lumps on the kitchen table. She reached out to take one. Miss Susan saw her and took down the whip. Harriet ran.

Years later, Harriet told the story of her escape from Miss Susan's house.

"I gave one jump out the door. I ran and ran. By and by, I came to a great pigpen. There was an old sow there and eight or ten little pigs. I tumbled over the high part of the fence and fell on the ground.

"And there I stayed from Friday till the next Tuesday, fighting with those little pigs for the potato peelings. By Tuesday I was so starved, I knew I had to go back…even though I knew what was coming."

Harriet went back. But she had grown too weak to work. Miss Susan punished her. Then she sent her home. Harriet smiled. The pigpen had been terrible, but it had felt good to be free of Miss Susan.

Harriet's Escape

Harriet did not want to be a slave all her life. "I will run away again. Next time," she said, "I'm going to go farther than the pigpen."

Her father told her, "Only the Southern states have slaves. If slaves run away and get as far north as Pennsylvania, they can be free."

"But the slave catchers are always watching. Runaway slaves have to hide by day. They have to travel north by night. They use the North Star to guide them," her mother said in a hushed voice. "They also use the Underground Railroad."

"What's the Underground Railroad?" Harriet
wanted to know.

Her father answered, "It's not a real railroad. It's
the name for secret paths north. The slave catchers do
not know about these secret paths. Some people help
slaves escape by the Underground Railroad. Their houses
are called 'stations.'"

"Maybe one day I'll be a 'passenger' and escape by
the Underground Railroad," Harriet thought.

When Harriet was twenty-four years old, she
decided to go north.

"Will you come with me?" she asked her family.

They were afraid. They knew that slaves who ran
away were often beaten or shot. No one would go north
with Harriet.

Harriet set out alone. She walked all night through the woods. The North Star helped her find her way.

Her first stop was nearby, in Bucktown. Harriet knew a white woman there. One day, the woman had whispered to Harriet. The woman had said that she was a "conductor" on the Underground Railroad. Harriet was sure the woman would help her escape.

"Here I am," Harriet said. "I ran away last night."

"Quick, take this broom and sweep the yard," said the woman. "This way, people will think you're my slave. You will be safe here!"

That night, the woman's husband hid Harriet
in his wagon. He drove her to the next town. He told
her how to find the next station. Her trip on the
Underground Railroad had begun.

For a long time, Harriet traveled by night. She slept during the day. She slept in attics, in haystacks, or in potato cellars.

On cloudy nights, she couldn't see the North Star. She knew that moss grows on the north side of a tree. She felt the trees to find moss. The moss showed her the way north.

Finally, she reached Pennsylvania. She was free.

"I looked at my hands to see if I was the same person, now that I was free," she said later. "There was such a glory over everything. The sun came like gold through the trees and over the fields, and I felt like I was in heaven."

The Underground Railroad

"I was free," Harriet said, "but there was no one to welcome me to the land of freedom. My home was down with the old folks and my brothers and sisters. But I was free, and they should be free. I would make a home in the North, and with the Lord helping me, I would bring them all there."

Harriet knew the slave catchers were always watching for her. But she went back to the South to get her family anyway. She became part of the Underground Railroad. The first slaves she led to freedom were her sister, and her sister's family.

But even Pennsylvania wasn't safe for long. There was a new slave law. All runaway slaves had to be sent back to their masters. Anyone who helped a runaway slave could be put in jail.

"We'll send our passengers north to Canada," Harriet said angrily. "In Canada, they'll be safe."

People who owned slaves wanted to stop Harriet. She was in danger every minute. But she kept going back to free more slaves. Sometimes she dressed as a man. Sometimes she wore a veil to hide her face.

Sometimes she played tricks. Once, she was sitting in a train station. There was a poster that told about her. It said that she had a scar. It also said that the person who found her would get a lot of money.

A man pointed at Harriet. He said, "She could be the woman the poster tells about."

Harriet couldn't read, but she picked up a book and held it open in front of her face.

"No, it can't be her," said another man. "The poster says Harriet Tubman can't read or write."

REWARD.
ESCAPED
SLAVE
Harriet Tubman

Another time, Harriet was walking down the street. She saw her old master. She had to think quickly.

She let go of the chickens she was holding. Then she bent down to chase them. She ran around in circles after the chickens. Her old master laughed. He did not see Harriet's face. He was too busy watching the chickens.

Harriet helped more than three hundred slaves escape by the Underground Railroad.

"On my Underground Railroad, I never ran my train off the track, and I never lost a passenger," she said. And she never got caught.

The Civil War

War broke out between the northern and southern states. Harriet became a nurse. She took care of wounded northern soldiers. She took care of southern soldiers, too.

Harriet still wanted to help slaves escape to freedom. She became a spy for the northern army. She went with northern soldiers to rescue slaves.

After four years, the North won the war.
Slavery ended. All slaves were now "forever free."

Harriet became a symbol of freedom. She fought
for what she knew was right. And she won her fight.